TIGER
WOODS

TIGER
WOODS

Jack Clary

SMITHMARK

This edition published in 1997
by SMITHMARK Publishers,
a division of U.S. Media Holdings, Inc.,
115 West 18th St.
New York, New York 10011

SMITHMARK books are available
for bulk purchase for sales promotion
and premium use. For details write or
telephone the Manager of Special Sales,
SMITHMARK Publishers, 115 West
18th Street, New York, NY 10011.
(212) 519-1300.

Produced by Belden Hill Press LLC
437 Belden Hill Road
Wilton CT 06897

ISBN 0-7651-9119-9

Printed in China

10 9 8 7 6 5 4 3 2 1

PAGE 1: Eldrick "Tiger" Woods, the
brightest new star among U.S. golfers,
with his third U.S. Amateur trophy.

PAGE 2: Tiger Woods at the 1996 U.S.
Open in Bloomfield Hills, Michigan.

PAGE 3: Tiger finished his U.S. Amateur
career in blazing fashion, winning his
third straight title in 1996 by coming from
five strokes down after the first half of the
championship round and winning on the
second sudden-death hole.

THIS PAGE: In 1996, Tiger Woods was
still two months shy of his 21st birthday
when he won his first PGA tour championship in his fifth tournament as a pro.

Contents

INTRODUCTION

Tiger Woods is a genuine American sports hero.

His face has graced the cover of many major magazines; profiles on his life have filled the pages of many others; there are several web sites on the Internet which track his every move; he was *Sports Illustrated*'s Sportsman of the Year in 1996; and he has had a profound impact on how the game is being played.

When he won the Masters golf tournament in 1997, he lit up the nation with his youth, good looks accentuated by a great smile, and awesome skill as a golfer. We sat transfixed watching him methodically win golf's most prestigious championship with incredible resolve and skill that could easily be appreciated without any intricate knowledge of the game. You didn't have to know the mechanics of the golf swing or how to handle a golf club to know that there was genius at work.

We like to believe that Tiger Woods represents the best we have to offer. A young man whose lineage encompasses five different nationalities, he has been raised by his parents with love and direction to become the best in his profession. That still is a work in progress that seems destined to succeed as no other in the sport's history.

While he is wealthy beyond all imagination, particularly for someone just beginning his twenties, he is not too self-important or caught up in material things that he cannot honor his parents with respect and admiration because they so honored him when he was growing up. They taught him a work ethic, insisted that he follow it and then cheered for him when he excelled and cried with him when he slipped.

Tiger has been compared to the best golfers ever to play the game, men who didn't reach the peak of their skills until they were many years older than Tiger is now. And while he is growing and improving his skills, his peers believe that he will influence the quality of his sport as no other golfer in history.

That alone sets him apart and makes him special in the way that all great performers are special.

OPPOSITE: Woods' great enthusiasm and charisma, punctuated by a gleaming smile, are as much a part of his golfing persona as his great skills on the course.

RIGHT: Tiger Woods was a national hero when he played in Thailand, his mother's native country. Crowds in Bangkok mobbed him during his victory in the 1997 Honda Classic.

PART 1

Tiger's Cub Years

Eldrick "Tiger" Woods was a child prodigy.

Child prodigies are usually identified with the world of music, playing a musical instrument with breathtaking talent or composing symphonies and sonatas at a very early age. Tiger Woods' talents are focused on the game of golf, but he was no less a child prodigy than Mozart, Beethoven or Gershwin.

How else could one explain the fact that he could handle a putter when he was just ten months old, when most youngsters are just learning to walk; or that before he was five years old, he could use a 5-iron to hit a golf ball as far as an adult could?

In fact, what Tiger Woods did as a young child is truly mind-boggling, and seems more the stuff of a Disney movie than of real life — a life that has become sport's most exciting new presence in a generation.

Without a doubt, Tiger Woods is the result of his father's plan to raise a golf champion. Earl Woods was a good athlete, whose principal claim to athletic achievement was as a baseball catcher during a short time at Kansas State University. Yet, his considerable physical abilities really blossomed while he was a member of the U.S. Army's elite Special Forces, the Green Berets, where stamina and skill, spiced with uncommon valor and resourcefulness, meant survival.

Woods was a career Army man who worked his way through the ranks to the rank of lieutenant colonel when he fought in Vietnam. It was during his time in Southeast Asia that he met and married his second wife, Kultilda Punsawad, who worked as a secretary at the U.S. Army installation in Bangkok, Thailand. Six years later, after his Army career had ended and he was working for McDonnell-Douglas in California, their only son, Eldrick, was born in Long Beach, California, on December 30, 1975.

Earl nicknamed his new son "Tiger" as a tribute to his dear friend and comrade Nguyen Phong, a lieutenant colonel in the South Vietnamese army with whom he had served in Vietnam and whom he had nicknamed "Tiger" because of his fearlessness.

Tiger is the product of a unique ethnic mix: His mother is half Thai, one-quarter Chinese and one-quarter Caucasian; his father half African, one-quarter Chinese and one-quarter Native American.

OPPOSITE: Tiger Woods is a mix of five different nationalities: Thai, Chinese, Native American, African-American and Caucasian. To describe his lineage, he coined the term "Cablinasian."

RIGHT: Tiger hugs his mother Kultilda after a tournament victory. She met and married Tiger's father, Earl Woods, while he was stationed with the U.S. Army in her native Thailand.

This mix would sometimes become a subject of contro-versy: when Tiger was a child, his father identified him-self and his son as African-American, but later, Tiger himself disavowed any specific lineage. In fact, he coined the term "Cablinasian" to describe his lineage.

Earl Woods had big plans for his new son, and they mostly revolved around the game of golf, to which Earl had been introduced a few years earlier. It is said that Earl broke 100 on his first round, broke 90 four months later and within five years, played to a 1-handicap. (Some golfers play their entire lives, spend a small fortune on lessons and trips to the driving range, and never break 90.)

Earl has said that he was driven by the fact that as a black, he had long been denied access to the country-club world of golf. "But I told myself that somehow my son would get a chance to play golf early in life." So before Tiger was even one year old, his father would take him out to the garage and put him in his high chair or playpen, where the boy would watch his father pound ball after ball into a practice net and putt ball after ball into a cup.

His father has said that when Tiger was just ten months old, an age when he still was being fed by his parents and having his diapers changed several times a day, he took up a putter and gave a perfect display of the delicate art of putting a golf ball. If this story is true, it brings the art of mimicry as a teaching tool to a new dimension — and indeed, mimicry is a valid tool for teaching young athletes the basics of a particular sport because they are so adept in their formative years at copying an instructor's precise body mechanics. If the instructor is a precision-artist in his skill, then the result is that much more perfect.

That seems to have been the case with Tiger. His father, even with his limited exposure to golf, had mastered the proper techniques and imparted them to his son. Thus, before Tiger was out of diapers, he was playing the Navy course in Los Alamitos, California; when he was three, he won a pitch, putt and drive competition against ten- and eleven-year olds; and at age four, he carded a 48 from the red tees at the Navy course at Cypress, near his home in California. He

was four-and-a-half when he made his first birdie, scoring two at the par-3, 91-yard third hole at Heartwell Park Golf Club.

But his father didn't limit his instruction to the sheer mechanics of golf. During his years as a Green Beret, he had learned a great deal about shaping a mind to cope with stress, and so he set out to mold his son's mind so that he could master the all-impor-tant skill of concentration. At age six, while Tiger was out in his family's garage hitting balls into the same net he had watched his father use, he was also listen-ing to subliminal messages on a tape recorder. His father had also tacked messages of positive reinforce-ment to Tiger's desk in his room.

At the par-3 course at Presidio Hills, while Tiger played, his father spent a couple of months using training methods he had learned as a Green Beret to assail his son with all sorts of psychological impedi-ments. The Green Berets had used explosive charges, ambushes and terrain obstacles; on the golf course, Earl Woods used a myriad of distractions — viola-tions of the gentlemanly rules of the game — that could cause a golfer's game to fall apart. His father did everything from making caustic remarks before Tiger was set to tee off or sink a putt to making noise at the top of his backswing. (Tiger showed that he could still be vulnerable at times when, on the 18th tee of his final round of the 1997 Masters, the click of a camera sent his backswing awry and caused him to slice his tee shot. Nonetheless, he recovered and made par on the hole.) In Earl's own words, he pulled "every nasty, dirty, ungodly trick on him." This went on until his father was satisfied that he could endure anything on a golf course and not crack.

Thus, anyone watching Tiger's steely-eyed determination from the time he began playing com-petitive golf through the methodical way he attacked Augusta National in the 1997 Masters and onward can see how adept he had become at overcoming most pressures and not allowing them to interfere with his game.

Still, his father has always maintained that he would not have objected if Tiger had one day sudden-

ly rebelled against this life and rejected golf as a serious avocation. "All we really cared about," he has said, "was raising a meaningful, articulate citizen."

He also admitted that there were times when his son was too obsessed with the game and with winning. Earl advised his son that there were other things to enjoy in life, but was slightly taken aback when Tiger told him that winning and shooting low scores was "how I have fun." His father never raised the issue again.

While Earl handled the golf course and the playing schedule when his job allowed, as well as juggling the family's financial resources to help maintain Tiger's playing needs, his wife provided strength and stability at home. She not only served as a taxi service to Tiger's mid-week golf matches, but more importantly, she also saw to it that he responded to all the demands of family life. She insisted that he comport himself properly, and particularly that he adhere to the gentlemanly protocols of golf. At the time, the unsportsmanlike behavior of tennis stars Jimmy Connors and John McEnroe and other sports figures were serving as poor role models for young, impressionable athletes. Tilda Woods wanted to make sure

that her son did not follow in those footsteps.

At the same time, she taught him some of her own toughness, driving home the point that when he was ahead in a match he should not let up but instead, try as hard as he could to overwhelm an opponent. Then, when the match was won, he was to be a sportsman.

The "tough love" that Earl used to shape his son's character was nothing more than solid parenting, although some might consider his methods harsh, since Earl Woods demanded a great deal of his son from a very early age. For example, he often told the story of Tiger, at age four, expecting his father to keep track of his golf clubs and put them into the car whenever they went off to hit some balls. Earl wanted to teach his son a lesson, so on one outing he hid the clubs under the front seat of the car. When they arrived at the course, Tiger asked his father whether he had packed his clubs.

"Why would I do that?" his father asked. "They're your clubs, they're your responsibility."

When he told the story on the *Oprah Winfrey* television show, Oprah was aghast and tried to make the point that Tiger was just four years old at the time, and certainly it was not unreasonable for his father to take care of his clubs.

"Why should I?" Earl Woods replied. "He had bought into playing golf, therefore he had to accept responsibility for all that went with it."

On the same program, Winfrey and Tiger discussed the downside of being a celebrity, particularly the harshness of the media. Referring to a story that appeared in *GQ* magazine just before the 1997 Masters, Tiger complained about the unfairness to him and his parents of being attacked by people he didn't know, and who obviously didn't know much about him.

His father, tough as always, brushed off the affront. "Life's not fair and these things are going to happen," he said.

And to be sure, the acorn named Tiger didn't fall far from the oak tree he calls "Pop." For example, in his very early years, Tiger was given a set of shortened clubs and when he looked in the bag and didn't see a 1-iron, the hardest club to hit, he asked to have one. He was told he was still too young to generate enough clubhead speed to use it effectively; but a while later, he was out on the driving range, using his father's 1-iron — which was almost as long as he was tall — so effectively that there was little doubt he could handle it. His dad promptly went out and bought him one.

Woods certainly could have become a "brat" because of his status as a child star had not the tough love that was part of his upbringing helped to short-circuit any potential problems. A Los Angeles television station ran a big feature on three-year old Tiger's golf prowess which then prompted the *Mike Douglas Show*, based in Hollywood, to give him national exposure when he appeared on the show with Bob Hope and Jimmy Stewart and showed off his putting style. A bit later, when he appeared on *That's Incredible*, with NFL star Fran Tarkenton, Tiger announced that he would beat Jack Nicklaus and Tom Watson "when I get big." His friends at school soon began asking for his autograph, which he had to print because he hadn't yet learned to sign his name.

When he was 11 years old, he targeted Nicklaus

as a golfing role model and the one he felt he had to beat to become Number 1. Tiger made a chart tracking Jack's career, writing a list of the major golf tournaments in one column, and in a second column the age at which Jack had won those tournaments for the first time. A third column was reserved for himself, to list the age at which he won those same events. "I wanted to be the youngest player ever to win the majors," he told *Sports Illustrated* a few years ago. "Nicklaus was my hero, and I thought it would be great to accomplish all the things he did even earlier than he accomplished them."

When Tiger was just 15 years old, he was asked to play an exhibition round with Nicklaus. Nicklaus had been scheduled to play with Phil Mickelson, the reigning U.S. Amateur champion, at a clinic during a benefit for the Friends of Golf at Bel Air Country Club in Los Angeles. But Mickelson couldn't make it, and the host for the event, Eddie Merrins, replaced him with Woods. Nicklaus knew of Tiger's reputation and was just as intrigued as everyone else to see him play. After watching him send soaring shots to the far reaches of the famed Bel Air course, Nicklaus complimented the young golfer: "When I grow up, I hope my swing is as pretty as yours." That afternoon in the Pro-Am tourney, Tiger reached Bel Air's monstrous 575-yard 14th green in just two shots — not even Nicklaus could match that — and continued to amaze all in attendance with his prowess.

The next day, he returned to Western High School in Anaheim and the school's golf team. Six years later, when he competed in the 1997 Masters, it was Nicklaus' style of play at Augusta National which formed the basis of his game plan to win the tournament.

While Earl Woods had been Tiger's early tutor, he was smart enough to know that others were capable of teaching his son even more of the game's fine points, and into Tiger's life came a series of mentors who shaped and perfected his game. The first of those was Rudy Duran, a golf pro at Heartwell Park in Long Beach, who became Tiger's teacher before Tiger was five years old and was smart enough not to

BELOW: One of Tiger's most invaluable assets during tournament play is veteran caddy Mike (Fluff) Cowan, who helped guide him around Augusta National when he won his Masters championship in 1997.

tamper with the tremendous natural ability that the boy exhibited in the form of near-perfect mechanics at age five and six. In later years, when Tiger was still in his early teens, Duran was convinced that young Tiger could beat some of the best players in the world, and that he would eclipse all of Nicklaus' achievements.

When Tiger was 12 years old, he started working with John Anselmo, a teaching pro at Meadowlark Golf Club in Huntingdon. One day, he astounded Anselmo by complaining about the way his ball spun backwards after it hit the green, not realizing that he had naturally mastered this highly prized technique to keep balls from skipping off the putting surface. Anselmo then helped Tiger to work on his course management skills, and showed him how to put his shots in the most advantageous places.

At the same time, he met Jay Brunza, a San Diego sports psychologist and a captain in the Navy. Having one's own sports psychologist had become all the rage at this time, particularly for athletes engaged in non-team sports where they are totally dependent upon their own physical and mental skills. It is said that Woods' first exposure to Brunza included a series of "mind tricks", after which Brunza invited him to join his golf group the next day at the Navy course. Tiger birdied five of the first seven holes, causing one of Brunza's group to ask: "What kind of monster have you created?" Brunza also used hypnosis to give Tiger positive reinforcement messages that got him into a "zone," and he continued using this technique after Tiger turned professional. Brunza also caddied for Tiger during many of his amateur tournaments so he could be instantly on-call.

Claude (Butch) Harmon Jr. was responsible for tightening up Tiger's swing off the tee and thus giving him one of golf's most formidable weapons. Harmon had been Greg Norman's coach and had helped make him the best driver in golf at that time. Earl Woods

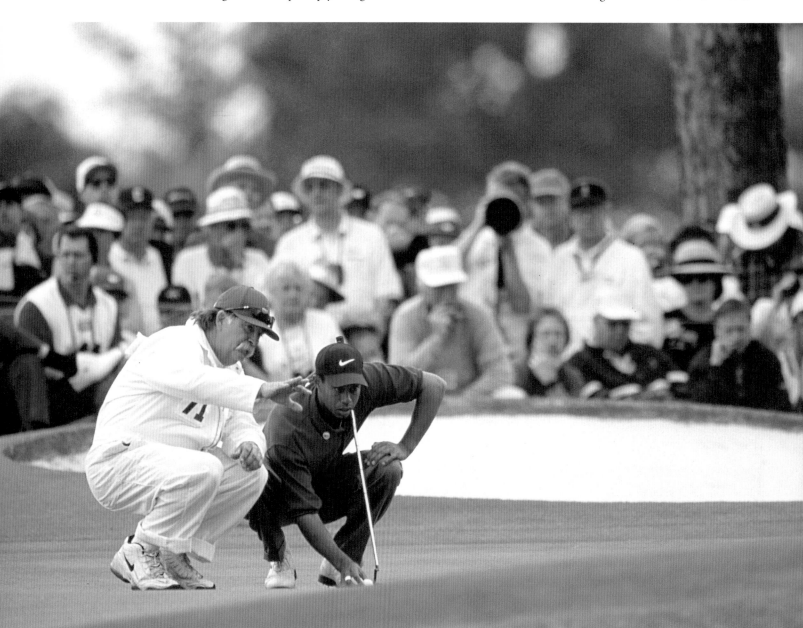

LEFT: Tiger prepares to play a practice round with two of the greatest golfers ever — Jack Nicklaus (left), and Arnold Palmer.

BELOW LEFT: Tiger had excellent teachers from his early years on, including Claude (Butch) Harmon Jr. (left); sports psychologist Jay Brunza (second from left); and his dad, Earl.

BELOW: Woods can't go anywhere without attracting crowds, even when he is among thousands of spectators at a basketball game.

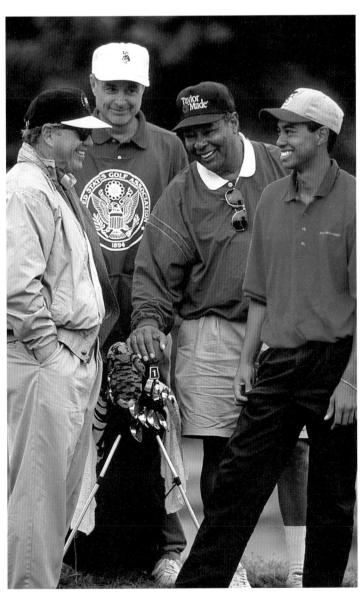

didn't hesitate to call him after Tiger lost the 1994 U.S. Amateur in Houston, and Harmon worked with Tiger twice, videotaping Tiger's swing and then breaking down the parts that needed to be changed. "Tiger showed me his shots, and I made some suggestions at the time that helped his consistency," Harmon said later. "It was nothing special but I guess he liked the results."

He liked them so much that although they rarely got together, rarely a week passed that Tiger didn't call Harmon for advice, and periodically he sent him tapes of his golf swing. He has remained Tiger's golf guru.

Tiger has always been smart enough to realize that he could not do it all by himself and that others with far more experience, in any number of areas, were assets from which he should draw. For instance, when he was teamed with the sport's great stars while still an amateur, he absorbed as much knowledge from them as possible as he peppered them with questions about all facets of the game. When his fame as a pro began to blossom even before he won the 1997 Masters, he consulted golf legend Arnold Palmer and NBA star Michael Jordan to find out how they each handled the overwhelming pressure of being a national celebrity.

Like many child prodigies, Tiger faced his own

particular pressures — his life was divided between elementary school and the adult world of golf. He knew how good he was and took some special delight in beating his father for the first time when he was just eight years old. His dad later told friends that once his son beat him, he knew that he never again would hold a mastery of the game over him.

All the while, Tiger kept improving. At age 10, he had already won two Junior World 10-and-under titles in San Diego but was unhappy about being forced to restrict his game and not being allowed to tee off with his woods on major courses. His father took him to the Navy course, but the members began to grumble and enforced a rule forbidding children under ten to play. Tiger believed there was some racism involved in that decision, and later noted that he had been allowed to play the course when he was four. "But all the members got mad because I was beating them."

While he was ascending in the world of golf, he still had to cope with the same everyday concerns as his friends. There was an iron-clad rule in the Woods home that there would be no golf until all of Tiger's homework was finished. Although he was traveling the country to play in various events, he also had to keep up with his schoolwork, and his father insisted that he take his books with him. He was able to juggle his two lives very well, and he maintained a 3.75 grade point average in middle school.

When he was invited to play in his first PGA event, the 1992 Los Angeles Open where he would be teamed with some of the nation's top golfers, he was not permitted to be absent from his classes at Western High School until he obtained a pass from the principal's office. In his senior year, he was enrolled in honors courses and maintained a 3.3 grade point average. Woods' high school golf coach, Don Crosby, who also taught him accounting for two years, said that his attitude and competitive nature in the classroom were no different from on the golf course or the practice area. "He was a very competitive young man who wanted to be the best no matter what it was. If he didn't get the top grade in the class, he studied even harder the next week. He was always goal-oriented and he never got off the track."

He concentrated on his schoolwork from fall to early spring, putting away his golf clubs in favor of running the 400-meter event on the school's track team (his best time was 52 seconds), and not even talking about golf unless his friends brought it up. In the spring, he resumed playing and often played in major amateur events out of town on weekends, returning to his schoolwork and competing as a member of Western's golf team during its scheduled midweek matches. As a freshman, he led his team to the Orange League championship, and he finished his high school competition by winning the state Southern Section individual championship. Earlier that year, he had received the Dial Trophy as the top male high school athlete in the nation.

One piece of sage advice Tiger received as a high school student came from Mark O'Meara, now one of his close friends on the PGA tour, when they played together at the 1992 Los Angeles Open. O'Meara sensed that Tiger might be too obsessed with the higher levels of golf, particularly since he would now

BELOW: Tiger's trophy room in his California home fairly bursted with the hardware that he had accumulated during his early years. He was just 13 when he played his first national tournament, and he actually led future PGA and British Open champ John Daly by five strokes at the halfway point of the third round before losing by two strokes. Still, he beat eight other pros that day and finished the tourney in second place.

be regularly invited to major events because of his success in the amateur ranks, and that he was looking for-
ward to the day when he would become a tour regular
without realizing that it is mostly business and responsibility. O'Meara told him "to appreciate that he's
going through the best years of his golf life" as a young
amateur and high school competitor, "and to have fun
and be as normal as he can be and enjoy his golf."

Yet the biggest lesson Woods learned came on
his 17th birthday at the Orange Bowl International
Junior Invitational tournament in Miami where he
was favored to win his eighth title of the 1992 season.
He started the final round tied with Lewis Chitengwa
of Zimbabwe, and was serenaded with a chorus of
"Happy Birthday" on the first tee. But Tiger's game
began to come apart midway through the front nine
and then so did his mental outlook, and he com-
ported himself badly the rest of the way, obviously in
a sulk because of his golfing problems. He lost
the match and had to win a playoff to get second
place. After the match, Earl Woods became a Green
Beret once more and reprimanded his son: "Who
do you think you are?" he said, in a tone of voice that
Tiger had never heard before. "Golf owes you nothing. The nerve of you quitting out there on the golf
course. You never quit! Do you understand me?"

From that day on, Tiger has never stopped
challenging for the lead, regardless of a deficit, and he
certainly has never believed any lead he had was
absolutely safe. To do otherwise is "giving up" by his
standards, and he simply couldn't face his father's
wrath one more time.

Yet, that was all part of the maturing process,
and he still was further ahead than most at his age.
A year earlier, when he was just 16, Tiger took stock
of his strengths and weaknesses, as a golfer and as a
person. The golfing part was easy because it dealt
with the consistency of his game; the personal part
was a bit tougher, because he looked at himself truth-
fully and found that his lack of maturity, physical as
well as mental, were his biggest drawbacks. His
physical growth continued to hamper his swing, and
until his body stopped growing, his swing would be

erratic. He further admitted that "16-year old problems" hampered his decision-making, where his emotions often overrode his reasoning and caused him
"to try things that aren't very smart."

He had to cope with his "weaknesses" on the
run, because he maintained a brisk schedule of tour-
nament appearances, including three in the U.S.
Junior Amateur Championship beginning in 1991 at
age 15. That year, which set a pattern right up until
he turned pro in 1996, he had already won the CIF-
Southern California Golf Association High School
Invitational Championship, the Southern California
Junior Championship, the Ping Phoenix Junior, the
Edgewood Tahoe Junior Classic, the Los Angeles City
Junior Championship, the Orange Bowl Junior
International and for the sixth time, the Optimist
International Junior World Title.

On July 28, 1991, he won his first national title
in his first appearance in the U.S. Junior Amateur,
becoming its youngest winner ever by winning a playoff against Brad Zwetschke. And for the first time,
he encountered the stunning pressures of tournament
golf; but with Brunza along as his caddy to provide
support, Tiger regained his composure and won on
the first extra hole, though he made bogey.

This blistering pace continued with two more
victories in the U.S. Junior Amateur and three as
U.S. Amateur champion, as well as a full load with
the NCAA champion Stanford University team and
beginning in 1992, regular appearances along the
PGA circuit as an invited amateur.

He also continued his regular high school student
life, and to keep things on an even keel, he passed
up U.S. Open qualifying in 1993 to attend his high
school graduation. He also later skipped the CIF-
Southern California Golf Association Championship
to play as an invited amateur in the PGA Buick
Classic in Westchester County, near New York City.

Yet, one thing never changed with Tiger Woods:
He never took his eye off his goal to be the best golfer
of all time, and he poured all of his talent and ener-
gies into this crusade as he began to climb the ladder
to become one of the nation's top golfers.

PART

From Amateur to Pro

Tiger Woods has declared that he always knew when it was time to move to the next plateau in his golf career: He started playing badly at the one in which he was competing.

Thus it was that he moved from the U.S. Junior Amateur championship ranks, after becoming the first to win three straight years, and into a higher level of competition that included the U.S. Amateur and allied events at that level; NCAA competition after he enrolled at Stanford University; playing in PGA events, including the Masters, plus the U.S. Open and the British Open; and finally plunging into his professional career in the late summer of 1996.

His progress in the world of golf was hardly a surprise, because he had carved out such an impressive record at a young age. In his early teenage years he had already been tabbed as the sport's next great star. He had played in competitive golf tournaments since he was in junior high school, so he was well-prepared for his move into tougher competition. If anything, he embraced the challenge, saying that it makes the game fun for him.

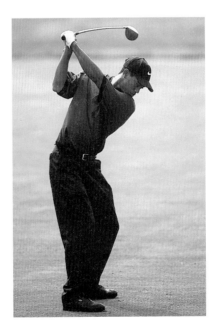

Mechanically, no golfer has been more perfect, and none can overpower him. Although he is long and lean — 6'2" tall and only 165 pounds — he has been compared in physique to former boxing champion Tommy Hearns. His biceps are generous and sit comfortably atop his 28-inch waist. His frame disguises the muscular strength that he has developed from playing golf and from a regular regimen of weight and resistance training that often includes squats with as much as 250 pounds and 500 abdominal crunches to strengthen his lower back against the force of his explosive swing rotation.

The key to his golf mechanics, according to his teacher, Claude (Butch) Harmon, Jr., is his swing, beginning with the position of his club at the top. "He has to make sure his swing is in the right position at the top," Harmon said. "If it's out of position — given his clubhead speed (130 miles per hour, about 75 percent of his capacity) — he could hit it anywhere."

His shoulders are past 90 degrees, and his hips turn only about 30 degrees. This combination creates his power, and Harmon likens him at this point in his swing to "a rubber band wound tightly." His

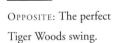

OPPOSITE: The perfect Tiger Woods swing.

RIGHT: Tiger tore up the U.S. Amateur circuit during his teen years and then turned pro in 1996. His first PGA event as a pro was the Milwaukee Open, after he had signed endorsement contracts worth an estimated $60 million. He shot a 7-under-par 277 but still finished a distant 60th.

strength is enhanced by a strong grip and a wide stance that provides a wide swinging arc and full weight shift. His position, grip, alignment and stance are considered perfect.

But the key to any golfer's success is mental stamina, and Harmon says: "He's like a sponge. He takes in everything you tell him. He's the hardest worker I've ever seen, and he's mentally tougher than any guy out there today, the toughest since Jack Nicklaus."

Woods honed all of those assets with his great love of practice and his drive to perfection, and then polished them under competitive pressures, first as

an amateur, and since late 1996, as a professional. There is little doubt that he benefited tremendously from his amateur experiences, foremost of which was winning a record three straight U.S. Amateur championships. None of them were wire-to-wire finishes, but each served to make him a better golfer.

His first title came in 1994 at the Sawgrass course in Ponte Vedra, Florida, when he became the first player in that event's history ever to come from as many as six strokes behind and win. He also became, at the age of 18, the youngest winner in the history of the nation's oldest golf event; and the first black player ever to win, making a prophet of his

LEFT: Tiger Woods was the most nationally renowned golfer on Stanford University's team when he joined in his freshman year. But he was not necessarily the best, because the team already had four All-America players after winning the NCAA championship the previous year. In his second year, he won the NCAA title.

father who said after the victory: "I told him after he won his first U.S. Junior Amateur title, 'Son, you have done something no black person in the United States ever has done, and you will forever be a part of history. But this is ungodly in its ramifications."

Tiger helped make it so. In the quarter-finals of match play, he was three holes down with five to play against 1986 Amateur champion Buddy Alexander, the golf coach at the University of Florida. Alexander was in the process of playing bogey golf but Woods got a great break when an errant tee shot into the famed island 17th green nestled in the rough just a couple of feet from the water. He saved the hole and came back and won.

In the 36-hole final round, against Oklahoma State junior Trip Kuehne, he trailed until the 35th hole — by six holes after thirteen holes, by five with twelve to play, and he was three down with nine to play. Tiger kept after him and finally evened the match at the 34th hole with a birdie. Then, he was back hitting a wedge at the famed island green, and instead of playing it according to form — hitting to the left side of the green — he aimed his shot to the far right of the hole. The ball struck and it spun onto the fringe, then into the rough toward the water and back again onto the green's collar just four feet from

the water's edge. He then sank a 12-foot putt and after a par at the 18th, had a 2-up victory.

"I knew if I just hung in there, sooner or later those putts were going to go in," he said afterward. "And they did," although he said he was even more pleased with his comeback from a six-hole deficit. He went to Newport, Rhode Island, in 1995, to the site of the first U.S. Amateur, and became the ninth player — and the first since the immortal Bobby Jones — to win back-to-back U.S. Amateurs, again with another wild finish. Once again, it was a comeback trip — George Marucci, his 43-year-old opponent, led him by three holes after twelve, and by two after nineteen, but despite a run of three birdies over a four-hole stretch later in the round, he still couldn't put Tiger away.

Woods had a one-hole lead going into the last hole and Marucci put his tee shot in position to make a birdie and possibly tie the match. But Tiger arched a 140-yard 8-iron shot to within 18 inches of the cup and sank a birdie of his own to win. Afterward, Earl Woods told all who would listen: "Before he's through, my son will win 14 major championships." Tiger wasn't thinking that far ahead just yet. "This one meant more because it showed how far my game has come," he said afterward, and as he thought about

OPPOSITE: At the Newport Country Club in Rhode Island, site of the first U.S. Amateur golf championship, Tiger shows off his second straight U.S. Amateur trophy in 1995. It was only the ninth time anyone had won back-to-back titles. Woods came from behind in the 36-hole final round to win.

BELOW LEFT: Tiger Woods became the first golfer ever to win the U.S. Amateur in three consecutive appearances, wrapping up his storied amateur career with another come-from-behind sudden-death win at Pumpkin Ridge outside Portland, Oregon. He stacked those three titles on top of three previous consecutive U.S. Junior Amateur championships.

it he became even more animated. "That shot at 18 — damn! That's the only shot I could get close, that half shot. I didn't have it last year."

In fact, Woods' game had progressed to the point that he wasn't flummoxed by playing a course that took away his great strength off the tees and forced him to keep the ball in play against a field of more experienced short-game players.

His third straight U.S. Amateur victory, in 1996 at Pumpkin Ridge near Portland, Oregon, was just as hair-raising — he was down by five holes after eighteen, and it took two sudden-death holes to defeat Steve Scott. He had won medalist honors for the first two rounds; scrambled from two down to win the 18-hole semifinal; and then thrilled some 15,000 fans, the biggest crowd to watch this tournament in 66 years, with some breathtaking play on the final 18 holes during which he shot a bogeyless 65 on a day in which he hit 28 of his last 29 greens.

With eight holes to play, Tiger laced a 350-yard drive on the 553-yard hole en route to an eagle that trumped Scott's birdie; with three to go and down by two, he got a birdie on the 34th hole; and did it again on the 35th to tie. They halved the 36th hole and the first overtime hole. But on the next one, a 194-yard par-3, Woods landed his 6-iron tee shot 12 feet from the pin but missed the birdie putt. Scott had put his ball into the rough, ran a chip 11 feet past the pin and missed a par-making putt. Tiger drilled an 18-incher that made him the only person ever to win three straight U.S. Amateur titles.

These momentous events took place during his two seasons playing for Stanford University, where he led the Cardinal to the finals of the NCAA team championship as a freshman and won the NCAA individual championship to cap his sophomore season.

Tiger became interested in Stanford when he was just 13 years old and tearing up the junior golf circuit.

RIGHT: Stanford University's golf team featured Tiger Woods (back row, fourth from left), but it was a power-packed unit in its own right. In his freshman year, Stanford lost to Oklahoma State in the first sudden-death play-off in the 90-year history of the NCAA event.

BELOW: Playing golf was just one aspect of Tiger's college life at Stanford. He worked hard to keep up with his schoolwork and maintained a 3.0 average.

He heard about Stanford while watching figure skater Debbie Thomas, a pre-med student at the school, win a medal in the 1988 Winter Olympics. At the same time, Cardinal golf coach Wally Goodwin wrote him a letter simply inviting him to inquire about the school if he was interested. To Goodwin's surprise, Tiger replied and clearly and succinctly told of his achievements and his aspirations, which included not only becoming a PGA player but also obtaining "a quality business education." They never lost touch and Goodwin, helped by Stanford's academic and golfing reputation and the insistence of Tiger's parents that he get a good college education, always had an edge in recruiting him.

At Stanford, Tiger joined an NCAA champion team that had four All-America players, although none of them were as well-known as him; and he brought his team more attention than it ever had received, at the expense of more distractions than it ever had encountered. At one point, Goodwin was getting as many as 50 interview requests a day. Stanford's intercollegiate golf team wasn't the only beneficiary of Tiger's college career. At Arizona State's Thunderbird Collegiate Invitation tournament, gallery ropes were installed for the first time ever to accommodate crowds, and marshals were assigned just to attend Tiger's group. "What Tiger is doing for us," said Auburn University coach Mike Griffin, "is like what Arnold Palmer did for the PGA tour back in the 1960s. He may take the spotlight away from everyone else, but look at the attention he's brought to our game. How can we complain?"

In Wood's freshman year, the NCAA handed out 80 media credentials for its championship playoffs; in his second year, it certified 225 media people, and another 116 organizations were faxed a wrap-up after each round.

Away from golf, Woods enjoyed college life — except for the night he got mugged on campus — and labored as hard as everyone else to keep up with the academic workload, maintaining a 3.0 average and even pledging the Sigma Chi fraternity. His parents had sent him to Stanford, albeit on a golf scholarship,

expecting that he would graduate and they put no pressure on him to concentrate on golf rather than his studies.

There were some ups and downs in his college golf experience. As a freshman, he led his team with a 71.35 stroke average, won two tournaments and had six other top-ten finishes. But Georgia Tech's Stewart Cink, the nation's top-ranked collegiate golfer, beat him four times in head-to-head play. A week before Woods played in his first Masters, Cink beat him in match play three and two, and upon completion of the 18 holes, he also had a 66-72 edge in the medal score. When Stanford played in the Palmetto Dunes Collegiate tournament at Hilton Head, South Carolina, Woods was in first place going into the 17th hole of the third and final round when he made a quadruple bogey 8 and finished with an 80, tumbling to 13th place.

And because he had written a diary of his Masters experiences in 1995 for two golf publications, he was declared ineligible by Stanford. That lasted for an hour. Later, he allowed Arnold Palmer to buy him dinner while discussing a future pro career, and he was tagged with a one-day ineligibility sanction that lasted until he repaid Arnold with a check. Palmer cashed it, too.

Woods helped Stanford defend its collegiate title at the NCAA tournament at Ohio State at the end of his freshman season, but in the first sudden-death playoff in NCAA history, the Cardinal lost to Oklahoma State. Tiger came to the tournament hampered by a sprained right rotator cuff and physically exhausted after playing in a dozen college tournaments, the Masters and the World Team Amateur in Versailles, France. He finished in a tie for fifth place in the individual standings, but had he sunk a birdie try on the event's last hole, it would have given his team a second straight title. The ball skimmed the cup's right edge and spun away, forcing the playoff.

In 1996, as a sophomore, he won the individual NCAA championship at the Honors Course in Chattanooga, Tennessee. He took the lead in the

RIGHT: Even with his full collegiate golf schedule, Woods played a heavy amateur schedule and used his amateur exemptions to compete in PGA events such as the J.C. Penney Classic in Florida in 1996.

OPPOSITE TOP LEFT: Woods' 71.35 stroke average led the Stanford golf team during his freshman season. He had two tourney victories and finished among the top ten in six other events.

OPPOSITE TOP RIGHT: Woods' presence put a great deal of pressure on his teammates at Stanford because of the constant media glare. Some believed that having to compete in such a fish-bowl environment affected their performance.

OPPOSITE BOTTOM: In the 1995 NCAA championship against Oklahoma State, Tiger sank the tie-making putt that sent the tournament into sudden death. The following year, he won the NCAA title with a four-shot victory over Arizona's Rory Sabatini.

ABOVE: Woods took a
nine-stroke lead into the
final round of the 1996
NCAA championship
but finished that day with
an 80, still good enough
to give him the title at
the Honors Course in
Chattanooga, Tennessee.

OPPOSITE: Woods was
the only golfer in the
NCAA field to break par
during the 1996 tourna-
ment. He shot a 67 on
the second day to break
the course record that was
held by three golfers,
including Gary Nicklaus,
Jack's son.

second round and had a nine-shot lead going into
the final round before skying to an eight-over-par 80,
and he still won by four shots. He was the only golfer
in the 156-member field to break par, and at the
awards dinner he reiterated that he would not turn
pro before he was due to graduate in 1998. He later
amended that to "unless something exciting happens."

Something exciting was happening at the home
office of International Management Group (IMG), the
worldwide sports marketing conglomerate that repre-
sented some of golf's biggest names and devised multi-
million-dollar endorsement deals with Fortune 500
companies. IMG had targeted Tiger since he was 12
years old and the head of IMG's golf operations division, Hughes Norton, had continued to display interest
by keeping in touch with Earl and Tilda Woods.

Tiger had nothing left to prove on the amateur

level. He had been a U.S. Golf Association champion
for six consecutive years, matching Bobby Jones'
record; and his place as one of the greatest amateur
golfers in history with his 18-0 record in match play
was very secure. A few weeks earlier, he had lost in
the first round of the Western Amateur which was a
tip-off to him that he was bored with this level of play
and it was time to move on. He won his third U.S.
Amateur and a few days later, on August 27, 1996,
at the Milwaukee Open golf tournament, Woods told
the world he was now a professional golfer.

No one was really surprised, despite the fact
that he had insisted that he intended to graduate from
Stanford before turning pro. He had already sought
and received the assurances of such pros as Ernie Els,
Greg Norman and Curtis Strange that he was ready
for the PGA tour. Butch Harmon said: "He's got the

RIGHT: Tiger used the mental discipline instilled in him by his father to good advantage when he disregarded sub-freezing wind chill conditions in a pro-am tourney before the 1996 Tour Championship at Southern Hills Golf & Country Club in Tulsa, Oklahoma.

BELOW: Woods won his second PGA event in 1996 at the Walt Disney World Golf Classic in Orlando. During one of his rounds, he reached the 614-yard eighth hole in just two strokes.

intelligence and the tools to succeed very quickly. My only worry is that he's losing two of the best years of his life to do something that is very demanding for a young person. Considering everything, he's making the right decision but he's going to have to grow up faster than I'd like him to."

When Earl Woods saw that his son was determined to make the move, he opened the most powerful bidding war ever for a pro golfer, one that eventually netted $60 million in endorsement deals that were brokered by IMG. His income goes into Tiger Woods Inc., of which he is chairman and his father is president. Of course, that instant wealth hasn't kept him from getting excited about winning "penny ante" golf bets which spices everything golfers do on a course.

His biggest concern was avoiding the tricky PGA Tour Qualifying tournament in early December, and to do that he had to be among the top 130 money winners, which was estimated at about $150,000. He chose a seven-tournament schedule to achieve the goal, and to the amazement of some, he did it quite easily. He won the Las Vegas Invitational, his fifth event, and the $297,000 first prize (he had entered with winnings of $138,000) and two weeks later, captured the Walt Disney World/Oldsmobile Classic and its $216,000 first prize. Counting in other events, in just four months, he totaled more than $940,000 in winnings and earned a two-year exemption from tour qualifying.

He didn't turn the pro golf world upside down immediately, finishing 60th in the Milwaukee Open with a seven-under-par 277. He was eight-under for a much-improved eleventh-place finish in the Bell Canadian Open, and then was jolted when he blew the tournament lead in the final round and finished in a fifth-place tie in the Quad Cities Classic, four strokes behind winner Ed Fiori. After starting strongly in the last round, his game came apart at the fourth hole and then his putting became erratic. It was like a collapse he had earlier in the year while playing as an amateur in his second U.S. Open at Oakland Hills, in Michigan, when he blew an early first-day

lead by losing nine strokes in the final five holes.

"I was shocked," Earl Woods admitted afterward. "I thought that reaction would be all over after the U.S. Open. But that was a first round, this was a final round. It's a new, valuable lesson."

After finishing in a third-place tie in the rain-shortened B.C. Open, Woods finally reverted to the exciting come-from-behind golf he had played as an amateur and won his first tournament as a pro, and with it easily surpassed the winnings minimum and earned himself a two-year tour exemption and an automatic bid to the 1997 Masters. Nearly six months later, he won a lifetime invitation with his Masters victory.

At the 90-hole Las Vegas Invitational, he shot 70 in the first round, then played the last 72 holes in 26-under-par, just a stroke off the PGA record for a regulation 72-hole tournament. He shot 64 in the final round and then beat Davis Love III on the first hole of a playoff.

Two weeks later, he won the Disney, his fifth top-five finish in his last five starts. Jack Nicklaus quickly put Tiger's presence on the tour into perspective: "I don't think we've had a whole lot happen on the tour in what, ten years? I mean some guys have come on and won a few tournaments, but nobody has sustained and dominated. I think we might have somebody now."

Still, it was a gritty performance because Woods fought the flu throughout the tournament and never allowed it to diminish his power. On one 595-yard hole, he was 284 yards from the hole, with trees and a lake guarding the green, but he struck a three-wood that sent the ball over the green. On a 614-yard hole, he reached the green in two strokes. Before he started the second round after opening with a 69, he told his father he needed to shoot a 63 — and he did just that, which even amazed his dad.

Everyone wanted to know what had transformed this young golfer, who had never finished higher than 22nd in any PGA event as an amateur. He had an easy explanation: "When I played in those tournaments, I was either in high school or college. I'd get

OPPOSITE: Woods lines up a putt during his first tournament as a pro at the Milwaukee Open. He won only $2,544 at Milwaukee with his 60th-place finish.

LEFT: Tiger displays the winner's trophy he garnered after beating Tom Lehman in a one-hole playoff in the 1997 Mercedes Championship.

BELOW LEFT: Woods with his winner's trophy after capturing his first pro title at the 1996 Las Vegas Invitational.

BELOW: Tiger ignores a driving rainstorm on the practice green at the 1996 Canadian Open.

BELOW RIGHT: Woods
with his mother Kultilda
after he won the Asian
Honda Classic in 1997
with a 20-under-par 168.
The event was played in
Bangkok, Thailand, his
mother's birthplace. Tiger
had to overcome heat
exhaustion that caused him
to miss the event's pro-am.
Still, tens of thousands
of Thais turned out for
the tourney.

dumped into the toughest place to play, and I usually was trying to study, get papers done and everything else. I knew if I came out here and played every day, I'd get into a rhythm, and I have."

Though he started the 1997 season by winning a rain-shortened Mercedes Championship in a playoff, nothing elated him more than not only playing in the Honda Invitational in his mother's native Thailand — the second time he had played in a tournament in that country — but also overcoming a case of heat exhaustion that forced him to withdraw from the pro am event, and going on to win the tourney with a final round 68. Tiger was an instant national hero in Thailand; his third U.S. Amateur victory in 1996 was replayed on national television six times within two weeks, and the final rounds of his victories at Las Vegas and Orlando were shown live, preempting NFL football.

While everyone was anticipating his first appearance as a pro in the 1997 Masters, he finished in a second-place tie with David Duval in the AT&T National Pro Am at Pebble Beach and recorded a ninth-place tie with Davis Love III in the Bay Hill Classic. Tiger got a taste of real golf life when he had to shed his shoes to play a ball out of the water at Bay Hill but true to form, he sent a 5-iron to the front fringe of the sixth hole and birdied it.

He also was learning other lessons, mainly those concerning how to cope with life under a very hot spotlight. Unlike his forays into tournament play as an amateur, and his life as a golfer at Stanford, he had no friends his age with whom to socialize on the PGA tour and when his father left for his California home on occasion, life got lonely. At Tiger's new home in Orlando, he sometimes socialized with superstar athletes Junior Griffey and Penny Hardaway.

He also became a juicy target for the media, particularly regarding the issue of race. The media insisted upon referring to him as an African-American, an issue that became thorny after he won the 1997 Masters championship and was referred to as that event's first African-American winner. Woods did not directly disavow the label, and in fact, on the day he won the event, he saluted other black golfers who had preceded him to the Masters. But a few days later, during an interview on national television, he insisted that he did not wish to be exclusively referred to as an African-American, but that he was proud

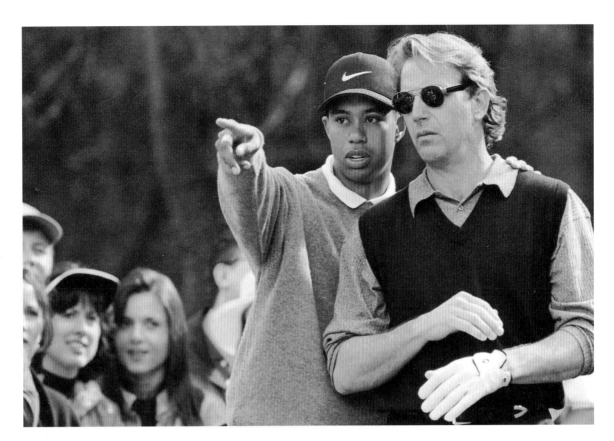

of his entire lineage and wished to be recognized as being the product of a multi-ethnic heritage.

He was very conscious of his impact on minority youth in America. During the Masters, he and his father put on a clinic at a nearby public course for a mostly minority audience. His presence itself served as great encouragement for minorities to begin showing more interest in the sport of golf.

Tiger also showed that he can be mature beyond his years when he took time off to be with his father after Earl had undergone heart bypass surgery. "The travel and the jet lag weren't that hard," he said. "What was tough was when my father was in the hospital. That's hard to deal with, I don't care who you are. I love him dearly."

Life on the tour, and in the high-powered endorsement world to which he has committed himself, continues to be a learning experience for Tiger even as he mesmerizes the golf world as well as those who previously had no compelling interest in the sport. Tiger is definitely his own man, refusing to be used or abused by any one constituency, while still growing in stature as an American sports hero, in the mold of basketball star Michael Jordan with whom he also plays an occasional round of golf. ("Make that two rounds at a time, and if Michael had his way, we'd play three rounds in one day," Tiger noted.)

"Now that I'm out here, I don't have to deal with the pressure of having to earn my card," he noted. "I put a lot of pressure on myself to make the top 125. It was pretty tough. I got through. I won twice in 1996 and I've won in 1997. But I'm still learning what my body can or can't handle, what my mind can or can't handle. I'm going to make decisions based on this and I may have to adjust my schedule to fit those criteria."

There is no telling how far he will go as a golfer but his future is unlimited. Record numbers of viewers around the nation saw that as they watched him dominate the 1997 Masters tournament as no golfer his age ever has.

It was a match for the ages . . . and it signaled that the Age of the Tiger had begun in earnest.

RIGHT: At a pre-tournament clinic, Tiger demonstrated his skill with his iron shots under the watchful eye of Fred Couples. Woods had honed his competitive skills by playing with some of golf's greatest shot-makers long before turning pro, absorbing every bit of help they had to offer.

PART 3

The 1997 Masters Championship

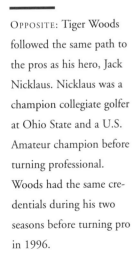

When Tiger Woods played in the Masters for the first time in 1995, he was low amateur and finished 41st, though he never broke par in any of the four rounds. During that tournament, he sat in the famed Crow's Nest, the room reserved for Masters champions, looked around, and displaying the brashness of a 19-year-old, exclaimed: "This place is perfect for me."

In 1996, Arnold Palmer, winner of four Masters titles, and Jack Nicklaus, who won ten, said after playing practice rounds with him: "Tiger will win more than the ten jackets we have accumulated."

In 1997, Tiger had his third opportunity to win the Masters, but only his first as a professional. Yet, as the tournament approached, Tiger was tired. The first three months of 1997 had been draining, with his father's illness and the pressures of tournament golf. At this time of the year in the past, he had been tired also, but that was because he was under the gun at Stanford, trying to cram for spring examinations, doing term papers, playing for his college golf team and traveling to special events on red-eye flights that taxed even the constitution of an energetic young collegian.

In the two previous years, he had been unable to

hone his game for this tournament, and that accounted in large part for his dismal showings (he didn't even make the cut in 1996). "The last two years [1995-96], I had to take finals the week before I arrived at Augusta," he noted. "That's kind of tough on you. But I didn't take finals last week. I didn't write papers. I was able to prepare for a tournament like I normally do."

He had circled the Masters in his psyche, and his steel-trap mind began to shut out all outside distractions and focus sharply on his dream of winning the most prestigious of all tournaments. The fatigue began to wash away as he methodically began to bring together all the elements he would need to fulfill the earliest of all his golf dreams. He stayed home in Orlando and worked on his game, tightened up his swing on his iron shots and worked on his putting, all the while constructing a game plan that would prepare him to the sharpest possible edge for the demands of the Augusta National course.

"All he has to do is play golf," his father said before the tourney began. "The idea is to keep everything free so he can do that. He goes into every tour-

---

OPPOSITE: Tiger Woods followed the same path to the pros as his hero, Jack Nicklaus. Nicklaus was a champion collegiate golfer at Ohio State and a U.S. Amateur champion before turning professional. Woods had the same credentials during his two seasons before turning pro in 1996.

RIGHT: Woods and Greg Norman were no strangers to each other in Masters play. They had played a practice round together in the 1996 Masters.

RIGHT: Before his 1997 triumph at the Masters, Woods' experiences in two previous outings at the event came as an amateur and were not very pleasant — he never broke par in six rounds, going 11-over-par. Still, he loved the atmosphere, and he told friends that some day his picture would be on the walls of Augusta National's clubhouse with other winners of the prestigious event. Woods is seen here with Tom Kite during a practice round.

nament with the express purpose of winning it, and this tournament is no different."

His parents' presence at Augusta, particularly that of his father, was perhaps his most formidable weapon. His father was still recovering from quadruple bypass heart surgery and post-surgical complications and was still so weak that he could not leave the clubhouse to watch his son play. Yet, he was available to give Tiger advice and serve as a psychological prop that kept him focused, and helped him to maintain the mental sharpness that is as important at this event as the requisite golf skills.

Still, the course as an entity, and the atmosphere which is the most charged in all of golf, was not exactly a stranger, though he had quickly found out that the Augusta course he had played in 1995 was not the same one he faced in 1996, nor would the one in 1997 be the same he had played in 1996. "They make subtle changes every year and you have to be prepared to alter your plan to suit the changes," he said. He also shrugged off his dismal showing in his two previous visits. "Well, don't forget, I was an amateur," he replied when reminded that he was less than spectacular in those six rounds. But after arriving at Augusta, he noted: "I feel comfortable just

because it's my third time here. I'm accustomed to it, I know what to expect."

Knowing what to expect of himself was equally important. In winning six U.S. Junior Amateur and U.S. Amateur titles, plus an NCAA crown, he knew how to peak for big events.

His playing style and Augusta National itself also meshed, particularly the four relatively short par-5 holes where score-shaving birdies were possible. They were easily accessible for his 300+- yard tee shots; his second shots were always high, soft-landing approaches which did not skitter into nasty places; and he also had a delicate touch around the greens to give himself an excellent chance for a bird (or even an eagle), and certainly get nothing worse than a par. Even when he missed a green, his deft wedge play gave him a chance to recover and be in position to make uncomplicated putts.

Woods didn't rely solely on his golf skills. He picked the brains of players such as Fred Couples, Ray Floyd, Nicklaus and Palmer, and he even went to the Golf Channel studios near his home in Orlando and watched tapes of previous Masters to study how past champions played the course. He liked Nicklaus' game plans best of all because he usually played the

FAR LEFT: Tiger plays a practice round before the Masters with golf legends Arnold Palmer (center) and Jack Nicklaus.

LEFT: Woods, seen here with caddy Fluff Cowan, struggled during the first nine holes of the first round in the 1997 Masters. He shot a 40 but he recovered with a 2-under-par 30 on the second nine.

BELOW: Tiger had to blast his way out of a sand trap on the second hole in the first round.

safe side of the par-3s and par-4s to set up easy putts, then lowered his score on the par-5s.

"That's the way I want to play," he said. "It's such a deceptive course. It looks wide open, but it's really got a pretty narrow route if you want to get a good angle on the pin. If you want to get your irons close, you usually have to land them away from the pins and in very tiny spots. I found that out the hard way in my two previous trips."

And that, by and large, is how he played his four rounds. He consistently boomed his drives over 300 yards to the right spot in the fairways. Mostly, his second shots were high, arching wedges, always conceding space to Augusta's greens and then allowing his putting skills to take over. He played the final 63 holes in 22-under-par; scored 13-under on the par-5s; and was 16-under on four tours of the back nine, bettering Palmer's record of 12-under in 1962, set 13 years before Woods was born.

He played a final tuneup round at the Isleworth Country Club in Orlando with Mark O'Meara and shattered the course record by shooting 13-under-par 59, going 10-under-par for the first nine holes. "It actually was pretty easy," he said later. "I did hit some bad shots, but they were only tee shots so I could salvage them."

Two days before the Masters began, someone asked defending champion Nick Faldo what chances the 21-year-old Woods, with almost minimal pro experience, had to win. Conceding that his achievements as both an amateur and a professional were "phenomenal," Faldo noted it took him personally about six Masters appearances before he could mount a serious charge, then said: "It's not impossible. But I think experience helps here. I wouldn't be shocked but it's his early days."

Then someone asked Tiger if it was realistic for him to think that he could win.

"To be honest with you," he replied, "I don't care what anybody else says. I just came here to win. That's what I'm going to do in every tournament. Is it realistic? I think so. I don't know if anyone else does. If things go my way, I might have a chance."

FIRST ROUND

Tiger Woods felt the butterflies when he stepped onto the first tee in the first round of the 1997 Masters. His playing partner was defending champion Nick Faldo, who had put on one of the most spirited charges in Masters history the previous year in overcoming Greg Norman's last-day, six-shot lead and winning by three shots. It was also one of the most notorious collapses in Masters history and forever let it be known that no lead ever can be considered safe on the Augusta National course.

And when both Faldo, who fought just to salvage a three-over-par 75 in the first round, and Norman, who had a 77 in the first round, disappeared from the field after two rounds, it also underscored that reputations are never a guarantee of success in the Masters.

All of the confidence and all of the skill that Woods had exhibited in the days before this event could not restrain the nervousness that gripped him, just as it did everyone else when they start playing in this tournament. That means that shots often fly where they're not supposed to fly; they often land in places long dreaded; and often the scramble mode becomes the operational method of playing.

It happened to Tiger. The greens were like ice-covered ponds, sending balls slipping and sliding in every direction, it seemed, except toward the holes which were located in places it seemed no man could reach. One golfer said, "Playing out here is like driving on ice. You've got both hands on the wheel, you're trying to be careful but you can't stop."

Woods was no different. As he warmed up on the driving range, he felt his swing was faulty. He was uncomfortable when he started out, and immediately was struck with a bad case of the hooks on his tee shots — the weapon that sets up his entire game — and sent four of them into the pine trees which line the fairways, beginning with the first hole. He duck-hooked his drive on No. 2, pulled the ball far to the left on No. 8 and snapped it off the tee at No. 9. "I was pretty hot at the way I was playing," he said later. "I couldn't keep the ball on the fairway. From

there I wasn't able to attack the pins you should attack. I was just playing real defensive golf, and that's not what you want to do when you're struggling. It was a tough day initially, but I got through it."

But not before he played a four-over-par 40 that included four bogeys, on that front nine. In addition to sending balls careening through the trees, he also flubbed a chip shot and lipped a three-foot putt. He had no feel for his clubs, for the ball, for the course. As he struggled, he became more frustrated and soon he was slamming his club disgustedly into the ground after each error.

"What was so frustrating was the fact that the fairways are wide open, but even so, I couldn't hit them," he said afterward. "I was driving bad and I knew what I was doing wrong. It was just a matter of getting out of it."

He finally did — in the space of time it took him to walk from the ninth green to the 10th tee by deciding to shorten his backswing and not make it so parallel to the ground — a drastic technical correction many golfers wouldn't even contemplate in the midst of a round for fear that everything would come apart and even their scramble mode would come undone.

"Sometimes you're lucky enough to find something that will right your game," he said. "I found it on the 10th tee box. I had been getting a little too long. I needed to get wider and shorter. From that position, I could zip the club on through. Pull it with my legs, not hit it with my hands."

And zip it he did. He ripped six strokes from par to finish the round with a two-under-par 70, and began the momentum that carried him to the most spectacular performance ever seen in a Masters tournament. He shot four birdies and an eagle, the latter on the par-5, 500-yard 15th by bending it to nothing more than a chip-and-putt hole after a mighty 379-yard drive. His wedge shot on the hole landed four feet from the pin.

His comeback really encompassed six holes:

10th: His eight-iron second shot landed within 15 feet of the pin and he sank the putt for a birdie, his first of the day.

12th: At the treacherous par-3 at Amen Corner, his wedge shot flew over the green but he chipped in his second shot for another birdie.

13th: He got another birdie after just missing an eagle 3 at the par-5 hole.

15th: His drive actually sailed into the crowd along the fairway, and as the spectators began dancing away to clear a path for the bouncing ball, it kept rolling another 100 yards down the hill and back onto the fairway, in perfect position for the wedge shot that he tucked next to the hole en route to his eagle.

17th: His second shot landed 12 feet from the

cup and following the advice of his mustachioed caddy, Mike (Fluff) Cowan, he took out a wedge and plopped it into the cup's right edge for another birdie.

18th: Even after his horrible start, Woods faced the possibility of breaking Augusta's back-nine record of 29 when his second shot landed 12 feet from the stick. But his putt barely slid past the hole and he settled for a par-4 and his 30.

His 70 placed him three shots behind leader John Huston after the first round.

When he faced the media after the round ended, someone asked: "Tiger, can you win the Masters?"

"I think I can."

SECOND ROUND

Proving that physical skills are important but that the mind can also do wondrous deeds, Tiger sharpened his game plan once he felt that his swing and the touch in his game had returned. He was relieved that he hadn't blown himself out of the tournament on the first day the way the favorites Faldo and Norman had done.

"The golf course was still playing awfully hard, and I had to be very patient out there," he said after shooting a six-under-par 66 for a 138 total, and a three-stroke lead over Scotland's Colin Montgomerie

and four better than Costantino Rocca of Italy, who were the two hottest European golfers at that moment.

"I played strategic golf. I fired away from a lot of pins and accepted two-putts, because par around here is not a bad score," he continued.

"And from there, if I drive the ball well, obviously, I may have a few opportunities where I can be aggressive. If I force the situation, I can make a bogey in a heartbeat. I was proud of the way I played. I didn't force anything today."

Nicklaus saw it in different terms.

"It's a shame Bob Jones isn't here," the six-time Masters winner declared, referring to the great legend who started this tournament and to whom both of them have so often been compared because of their successful amateur background. "He could have saved the words he spoke about me in '63 for this young man because he's certainly playing a game that we're not familiar with."

Part of the aura of the Masters, as Jones always said, is that history is bigger than any one player. That was before Woods, who was simply too long and too powerful for Augusta National on this day, causing Nicklaus also to note: "He makes this golf course into nothing."

His success was not totally centered on his prodigious driving ability, either. "Drives can go awry," Woods said. "My mind has always carried me to the winner's circle."

Still, the thousands who watched in person and millions more who saw his efforts on cable TV were awestruck when he hit drives to places no one had ever visited off the tee. He averaged nearly 337 yards per drive, missed only one fairway and needed just 29 putts. Tiger was five-under-par on the four par-5 holes, playing his second shots with short-irons that most golfers generally use for second shots to reach the shorter par-4 holes.

"The par-5s are good, and there are the par-4s where I'm hitting a lot of wedges," he added. "That's a big advantage."

Unlike the first day, he went right after the course, and simply erased any mistakes. But, he said, there was no continuation of his first day's play. "I had to go out and shoot a good number." he said. "But I hit the ball just like I did on the back nine yesterday in stretches . . . Some close shots; some sketchy shots but they weren't too bad. But I hit in the right places so I could either get up and down, or two-putt."

No. 2: On the 555-yard hole, he hit his second shot, a six-iron, into the gallery and then flubbed a chip. Still, he chipped in his fourth shot from 12 feet and got a birdie.

No. 3: His drive on the 360-yard hole landed within 15 yards of the stick and the return was easy.

No. 5: Tiger used a sand wedge from the fairway to get within two feet of the pin, and then polished off another birdie.

No. 8: He got his third birdie using his driver, then a 4-iron to get within 30 feet, and two putted.

No. 9: He got lucky after he hooked his drive into the pine needles along the fairway, and saw the spectators save a scorching low, punch shot, as the ball stayed on the fringes instead of sailing well past the hole. His 35-foot putt rolled eight feet past the cup but he sank the par-saver, punctuating this close call with his trademark pumped fist.

While that was certainly impressive, his power display on the back nine was awesome, causing Montgomerie to note: "On my drives, I'd like to hit his."

No. 11: He hit his tee shot 350 yards and needed only a sand wedge for the remaining 105 yards as part of a three-hole run of par golf.

No. 13: He eagled the hole with a three-wood off the tee, hit an eight-iron 170 yards, 20 feet past the cup and drained the ensuing putt.

No. 14: A birdie after hitting a 115-foot sand wedge to within three feet of the hole.

No. 15: Another birdie when his wedge shot sailed 159 feet, landing eight feet from the hole for an easy two-putt effort.

His only mistake of the day was a bogey on the third hole, the last one he shot for the rest of the tournament.

And what did he do when this fine round had

OPPOSITE: Woods' blistering play put more experienced former champion Nick Faldo (right, striped shirt) out of the running. Neither Faldo nor favorite Greg Norman made the cut after the second day. Tiger played the four par-5s in 7-under-par during the first two rounds, helping him shoot a 6-under-par 66 in the second round. He became the youngest player ever to lead the event at the halfway mark.

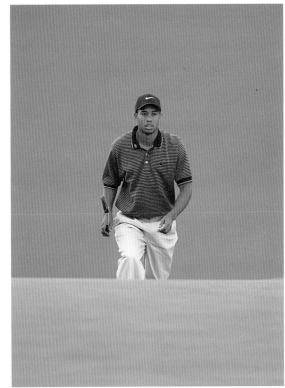

ended? He hit two bags of balls at the practice range, then had to explain to the scores of disbelieving media he had kept waiting that he never is satisfied with a round and that he practices so he can improve.

"He's playing a different course," said first-round leader Huston.

"He could become the first Masters champion who doesn't even shave," joked his playing partner, Paul Azinger, who fired a 73, and in his own words, "got smoked."

For his last 27 holes, Woods was 12-under-par and had without question turned the fabled Masters Golf Tournament into the Tiger Woods Show.

THIRD ROUND

Colin Montgomerie, who was paired with Tiger Woods for the third round, was discussing his opponent before they teed off.

"The way he plays, this course tends to suit him even more than anyone else playing right now. It depends on him. If he decides to do what he is doing, more credit to him," the red-haired Scotsman observed. "But at the same time, there's more to it than hitting the ball a long way, and the pressure's mounting now more and more."

Asked what edge, if any, did he have against Woods, Montgomerie replied: "I've got more experience, a lot more experience in major golf than he has and hopefully, I can prove that."

Alas, Montgomerie wound up a jittery, shaken wreck after walking 18 holes with Woods, who fired a superb seven-under-par 65, the second straight round in which he had the lowest score and a stroke better than his second-round 66 when he became the youngest player ever to lead the Masters. All of this gave him a record-making and untouchable nine-stroke lead while Montgomerie was blown away with his five-over-par 77.

Tiger was rewriting the record book. His 131 over his last 36 holes was a record, and his 15-under-par tied Ray Floyd's 54-hole total in 1975. When Woods finished the next day, he also buried Jack Nicklaus' 1965 record of 17-under-par for the tournament.

Still, he would not concede that he was playing his best golf. "I'll have to say this is as comfortable as I've ever felt. I'm thinking well and I'm playing well but definitely not the best ever," he said.

"He is a boy amongst men showing the men how to play," said Tom Watson, who had shot a tidy three-under-par 69, but still was 11 shots behind Tiger.

Jeff Sluman, the 1988 PGA champion who was a dozen shots back, jokingly suggested that the tourna-

OPPOSITE: Woods shot a 7-under-par 65 in the third round, giving him a nine-stroke lead. In the history of the Masters, it was the largest advantage that any leader ever held going into the final round. So overpowering were his tee shots in this round that he was able to use his irons and wedges to hit his second shots on the four par-5 holes. He birdied three of them.

ABOVE LEFT: Woods' play in the third round caused Jack Nicklaus to remark, "He reduced this course to nothing." Even so, when his round was finished, Tiger headed to the practice tee because he was dissatisfied with his game.

ABOVE: Tiger matched Ray Floyd's 54-hole Masters record of 201 after he shot a bogeyless third round and notched seven birdies.

ment would be more competitive had Tiger stayed at Stanford and not turned professional.

"I wish he had stayed in school and gotten his Ph.D.," Sluman joked.

Once again, Woods used his power off the tee and eased his way around a very chastened Augusta National course, helped by an overnight rain that softened its surfaces, en route to setting a record-tying 54-hole record of 201, 15-under-par. The longest club he used for a second shot on any par-4 hole was a 7-iron at the 485-yard No. 10.

Looking on, Jack Nicklaus remarked to *New York Times* reporter Larry Dorman: "People say the same things about him they used to say about me. I used to be sitting down there with 9-irons and 8-irons when everyone else is back there with 3-irons and 2-irons, and I was sort of laughing and snickering, saying, 'Boy, this is a tough course, huh?'"

For the second straight day, Tiger missed just one fairway and was eminently pleased with the strategy that such power produced — an average of 337 yards per drive that enabled him to fly past and over bunkers and other obstacles meticulously placed to harrass someone with lesser power. "With my drives, I can be aggressive," he said. "I can spin the ball, hold my distances a lot — I'll say a little easier than the guys who hit 7-irons on some of those par-4s. That's a great advantage and right now I'm really capitalizing on it."

This was instrumental in his birdieing three of the four par-5 holes — he was 10-under-par after playing 12 par-5 holes in three rounds — where he used wedges to ease his shot onto the green.

Ironically, his sand wedge became his deadliest weapon but only from the grass, because he stayed out of Augusta's numerous sand traps all day. Only at the 484-yard 13th did he miss, driving into the trees on the right but recovering with a 40-foot chip shot which Cowan, his caddie, called "the best shot I've ever seen," to help him par the hole.

Woods was just as proud of the shot. "I had a spot as big as a table to land the ball into," he said. "And then I had a little sand wedge, nipped it just

before it struck the ball. It hopped into the fringe and rolled onto the green. I thought it was probably the best shot I've played all week, considering how difficult it was."

His putter was just as torrid. He did not ram balls into the hole but he sent them unerringly toward the cup with a feather touch that slowed them to a crawl before they lazily plopped into the cup. He noted the par-3 16th hole which he parred. "It was an eight-footer which you should make every time," he recalled. "I'm just trying to get it close, and hopefully it crawls into the hole. That's the mindset — you have to have to putt well in Augusta, and so far it's working."

What helped was correcting a putting flaw his father detected just before Thursday's opening round. Tiger immediately went to the practice green and solved the problem. Then he went out and made two good par-saving putts on the first three holes, rolling in a four-footer on No. 1 and an eight-footer on No. 3 before kicking his game into high gear:

No. 2: After a strong drive down the left-hand side of the fairway left him 186 yards from the hole, Woods hooked a 9-iron over the green but scrambled back to tap in his second putt for a birdie on the par-5, 555-yard hole.

No. 5: This par-5 is considered Augusta's toughest hole but after a solid drive, Tiger hit a little wedge shot onto the green and capped the hole with a 15-foot putt.

Nos. 7 & 8: He birdied both holes. On the seventh, he hit a 2-iron off the tee, a sand wedge to within 12 feet below and to the right of the hole and sank the putt. On the 534-yard, par-5 eighth, he used his driver off the tee, then stroked what he later called "the best 2-iron hit I've made in a long time" 256 yards to within 20 feet of the pin and got down in two putts.

No. 9: Talk about the Luck of the Tiger? His drive sailed into the woods and he slammed the club into the bag, certain he was laying behind some huge pine tree out of sight of the green. Instead, the ball had carried the trees and stopped in perfect position

for his second shot to the green. He ended up with a two-foot putt to salvage par.

No. 11: Another birdie . . . and some more luck. Woods' drive sailed far to the right and into the rows of spectators, grazing the head of one spectator and bouncing through the legs of another before coming to rest on the edge of the fairway. He sent a 9-iron 143 yards to within 10 feet of the cup and sank the birdie putt, as the huge crowd exploded. Their reaction caused him to drop the expressionless mask he had worn all day and his face lit up with one of his patented toothy smiles.

No. 15: His drive down the left side landed by a tree and left him with no straight-line shot to the green. So he aimed a 6-iron at one of the bunkers, but with enough pull to land it on the back edge of the green, 35 feet from the hole of this par-5. Two putts racked up his sixth birdie of the day.

No. 18: Tiger crowned this glorious round with

his seventh birdie. The key was landing a sand wedge shot 106 yards onto the green and within a foot of the cup where he tapped home an easy putt.

Afterwards, Woods evinced surprise that nobody made a run at him and cut down his lead. "I told my pop before I left someone was going to make a run, shooting at least a 66," he said without noting that it was he who shot the day's low round of 65.

The closest anyone came was Tom Kite, who birdied three of the first four holes, and Costantino Rocca, who scored a roller-coaster 70 to ease into second place.

Someone asked Colin Montgomerie about the possibility of Woods replicating Norman's collapse from a six-stroke lead in 1996 to allow Nick Faldo to roar to the title.

"Nick Faldo is not laying in second place," the doughty Scotsman said, "and Greg Norman is not Tiger Woods."

LEFT: Just after he had bogeyed the fifth hole in the final round — his first bogey in 37 holes — Tiger composed himself and lined up a par-making putt on the sixth hole and continued his record-setting march to the title. "He turned Augusta National into a very short course," said two-time Masters champion Tom Watson.

FINAL ROUND

Tiger Woods had a sense of history and he was very aware of the significance of his nine-stroke lead as well as what it would mean when his name became attached to the litany of "firsts" that would be recited after his victory.

"It means that no one else has ever accomplished it, whether you were the youngest to win the Junior (amateur title) or the first to win two or three in the U.S. Amateur," he said before the round. "That means a lot to me."

The fact that Woods had such a commanding lead and that everyone all but conceded the Masters to him even before the final round began was a bit stupefying to him. In his boyhood dreams, he played against Greg Norman or Nick Faldo with just a stroke separating them, winning the Masters on the last hole.

Of course, it didn't happen that way because Tiger went out and buried Augusta National once more, shooting a three-under-par 69 for a record-setting 72-hole score of 270, 18 strokes under par. He became the youngest ever to win the title as well as the first to win the first major he ever played in as a professional. (The other "majors" are the U.S. Open, the PGA Championship and the British Open.)

Woods' 12-stroke victory margin was the largest ever at the Masters, shattering the shared record of nine strokes held by Jack Nicklaus and Raymond Floyd; and his victory margin was the largest in any major championship this century.

When he sank his final putt to make par on the 18th, he spun around and churned his arm up and down, his patented punctuation mark to signify that he had achieved something special. A few moments later, he was in the embrace of his parents, dissolving

into tears as he hugged his father for nearly a half minute. "I think more than anything I was relieved it was over," Tiger said later. "I think every time I hug my mom or pop after a tournament, it's over. I accomplished my goal. And to share it with them is something special."

When he talked by phone with President Bill Clinton a few moments later, the First Golfer told him: "The best shot I saw all week was the shot of you hugging your dad."

Tiger's last bit of good advice came from his father the previous night. "'Son,' he told me, 'this will probably be one of the toughest rounds you've ever had to play in your life. If you go out there and be yourself, it will be one of the most rewarding rounds you've ever played in your life.'"

"And he was right," Woods said. "It was very tough initially because I had to deal with a lot of different emotions, a lot of different thoughts going through my head; and I had to sort them out and execute the shots. I think the par I made on the first hole was really good; the up and down I made on 2

really got me going. I said, 'Okay, this is it. I'm going to stick to my guns and execute my game plan.' And it evolved into a victory."

His game plan for the last round was simple. He wanted to stay away from bogeys, which meant he also had to be patient. There was no need to attack the course and he believed that his chance for birdies lay on the par-5 holes. He did just that on three of the four holes and for the tournament, played the par-5s in 13-under, once again proving the adage at Augusta that the dividends for victory lay in those four holes.

Before, during and after the last round, everyone wondered just how Woods would keep his concentration at a peak when he knew he had wrapped up a victory. There was a blip when he bogeyed the fifth and seventh holes to "slip" to 24-under-par. But he soon recovered the skills that had brought him to that point. His round was not as dominating as those on Friday and Saturday, but only by a little bit:

No. 2: His birdie right off the bat, set up by a second-shot 8-iron to within inches of the fringe and

LEFT: Tiger Woods does his patented victory arm pump after sinking his final putt on the 18th hole that clinched the 1997 Masters championship. At 21 years of age, he was the youngest player ever to win the event, and he did so with a record-setting 270 over the four rounds. After shooting a 4-over-par 40 on the first nine holes, he was 22-under-par for the last 63 holes.

RIGHT: After winning the 1997 Masters, Tiger embraces his father as his mother (in the white-brimmed hat) looks on. Their reaction following the victory was very emotional, and spoke volumes about the close family relationship that has been an integral part of Tiger's success.

BELOW: Hail to the Tiger. The record-setting crowd at Augusta National salutes Tiger Woods after he sank his final putt of the 1997 Masters.

then a chip shot to within four feet of the cup.

No. 8: Another par-5 hole, another birdie. After pulling his second shot 4-iron to the trees on the left, he played an excellent pitch-and-run shot with his 8-iron over a mound to within four feet. The putt was automatic.

No. 11: The start of Amen Corner. "I knew I had to get through Amen Corner in even par at the worst, I couldn't let up," he said later. "I had to keep my intensity and concentration because you could hit a few balls in the water." He started with a birdie on the par-4 hole with a second shot wedge that put him about 20 feet to the right of the hole and beyond it. He curled in his second putt to go up by 16 strokes.

No. 13: After just missing another birdie by two feet on the 12th, he got one on this hole after unloading a tee shot 300 yards down the fairway, then exploding a 6-iron more than 180 yards, landing it six feet above the hole. He got down easily in two putts, just missing an eagle-3 by a couple of inches.

No. 14: His first Green Jacket was brushed off one last time after he racked up another birdie. Once again, his tee shot, a 3-wood, covered most of the 405 yards, followed by a lofted pitch with his sand wedge that hit the back slope and spun back to within eight feet of the cup. He easily sank his second putt.

No. 15: Proving he still is human, and that his concentration had begun to flag just a bit with the tournament in the bag, Tiger played scatter-shot on the 500-yard, par-5 hole. He pulled his tee shot to the 17th fairway, sailed his 5-iron into the gallery on the right of the green and then played more bump-and-run with an 8-iron that scuffed the ball just over the fringe and onto the green. His putt for a birdie rolled ten feet past the cup but his par putt was dead-on.

No. 16: He played it safe on the 170-yard par-3 hole. His iron shot landed on the back of the green, opposite the pin, and he tried to use the slope to loop his putt into the hole. It rolled about six feet past, but he calmly sank his second putt. "Once I got past the water holes, past 16, I knew it was pretty much over," he said later, "and that I could bogey in and still win."

BELOW: With the leader board as background, Tiger Woods lets his emotions flow as he finishes his record-setting 1997 Masters victory. The board doesn't tell the whole story, however — his 12-stroke edge was the widest margin of victory in Masters history. Some of his other records included a low middle 36 holes (131); low first 54 holes (201); low final 54 holes (200); highest under-par for the second nine (16-under-par); and most 3s on a winner's card (36). "This is a tournament that he probably can win for the next 20 years," said pro Tommy Tolles.

No. 18: This is supposed to be the victory walk for the leader; in Woods' case, it was a march of absolute triumph to celebrate his tremendous achievements at Augusta National and his face was lighted up with a huge victory smile as he strode onto the 18th tee. But it was not quite over yet. An over-zealous photographer clicked his camera at the top of Tiger's backswing and two more times as he brought his tee shot downward, causing him to flinch and hook his shot wildly to the left into an open area, 132 yards from the green. For a moment he glared at the photographer, then set off for his ball, and soon wound up joking with the crowd as marshals cleared a path for his second shot. He sent a wedge 30 feet past the pin, and took his shortened victory march, smiling broadly and tipping his hat to the crowd who saluted him with a deafening ovation. He quickly got back to business, looking at the spot of his ball and thinking: "Gee, I've got a tough one." Two putts later, he was the Masters champion.

While all of this was worth $486,000 and the title was his fourth on the PGA tour in just 15 events in less than a year, Tiger took particular satisfaction from his preparation before he arrived but even more in his own quiet work at the course itself.

"I've been able to practice the shots I've made at Augusta because this is the only place you can experience them," he said. "You can play bump-and-run at home but it does no good because the green speed is totally different from what we have to face out here. So when I come out here, I spend a lot of time chipping and putting off the greens. I spend a lot of time around the greens, and it pays dividends."

"I've never played an entire tournament with my 'A' game," he added. "This week, I came pretty close, 63 holes, excluding the first nine. This golf course can take anyone who is confident and humble them. I played pretty shaky on Thursday starting out, but from there it evolved into one of my best ball-striking tournaments."

There was one other bit of very personal satisfaction. Tiger was the first minority player ever to win the Masters, and he said his thoughts as he made his triumphant walk down the 18th fairway were of men such as Charley Sifford and Lee Elder, black golfers who had struggled to make the sport an all-inclusive game. "I said a quiet prayer of thanks for all that they had done to make it possible for me to be here," he said. Elder, the first black golfer to play at Augusta, in 1975, came from his home in Florida (and even got a ticket for speeding from a state policeman who, Elder said, didn't know about Tiger Woods) just to be present for Tiger's final round.

Elder hugged Woods when the tournament ended, and tears of joy streamed down Elder's face as he contemplated all that had happened. "I've not been this happy since I qualified for our country in the 1979 Ryder Cup," he said. "Tiger Woods winning the Masters might have more potential than Jackie Robinson breaking into baseball. Now, no one will turn their heads when they see a black walking to the first tee."

The entire golf world was agog as they contemplated what Woods had accomplished.

Tommy Tolles, who also was playing in his first Masters and shot a 67 in the final round to better Woods' score by two strokes, had it figured out.

"This is a tournament that he can probably win for the next 20 years," he said. "The rest of us will just be turning up for silver medals. We're all going to have to work to become better at certain aspects of our game because Lord knows, no one can hit it farther than he can."

British Open champion Tom Lehman may have summed it up best when he said: "I think Tiger's performance has got everyone feeling they have to improve or get left behind . . . . He is the prohibitive favorite for as long as he lives."

When Woods faced the media, someone asked him if he will become the greatest player ever.

"I don't know about that," Tiger replied. "But I know my goal is obviously to be the best. I know that's a lofty goal, but I think that if I try to accomplish that goal, great. If I don't, I tried. I expect nothing but the best for myself. And I think as time goes along, hopefully, that will happen."

OPPOSITE TOP: Tiger gets some help from 1996 winner Nick Faldo as he dons the coveted green jacket presented to each Masters champion. "It was something I always dreamed about. It's something any youngster who has played golf has dreamt about," he said.

OPPOSITE BOTTOM LEFT: Woods and Faldo, the 1997 and 1996 Masters champions. British Open champion Tom Lehman noted: "Tiger is the prohibitive favorite for as long as he lives."

OPPOSITE BOTTOM RIGHT: Woods flashes his great smile after winning the 1997 Masters. He also was the first minority golfer ever to win the event, and afterward, he paid tribute to other trailblazers such as Lee Elder, the first black golfer to play in the event.

Index

Photo Credits